☙ REVIVAL ☙

A Writer's Journal

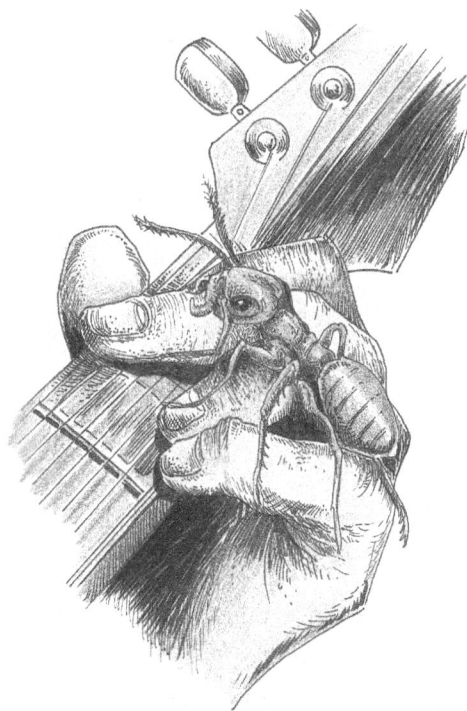

OVERLOOK **C**ONNECTION **P**RESS

2016

Revival: A Writing Journal
© 2016 by Overlook Connection Press.

Dust Jacket & interior Illustrations © 2016 by Glenn Chadbourne.

This is a blank journal, featuring lined pages for you to write your personal
or work information. This journal will help with your writing no matter
where you are, to help keep a steady hand.

A portion of the proceeds, from the sale of this journal, are donated
Stephen King's Haven Foundation for authors and artists.
Learn more about how you can help the Haven Foundation at
thehavenfdn.org

Published © 2016 by
Overlook Connection Press
PO Box 1934, Hiram, Georgia 30141
OverlookConnection.com
StephenKingCatalog.com
overlookcn@aol.com

ISBN: 9781623300814

1

2

4

5

6

13

28

29

58

71

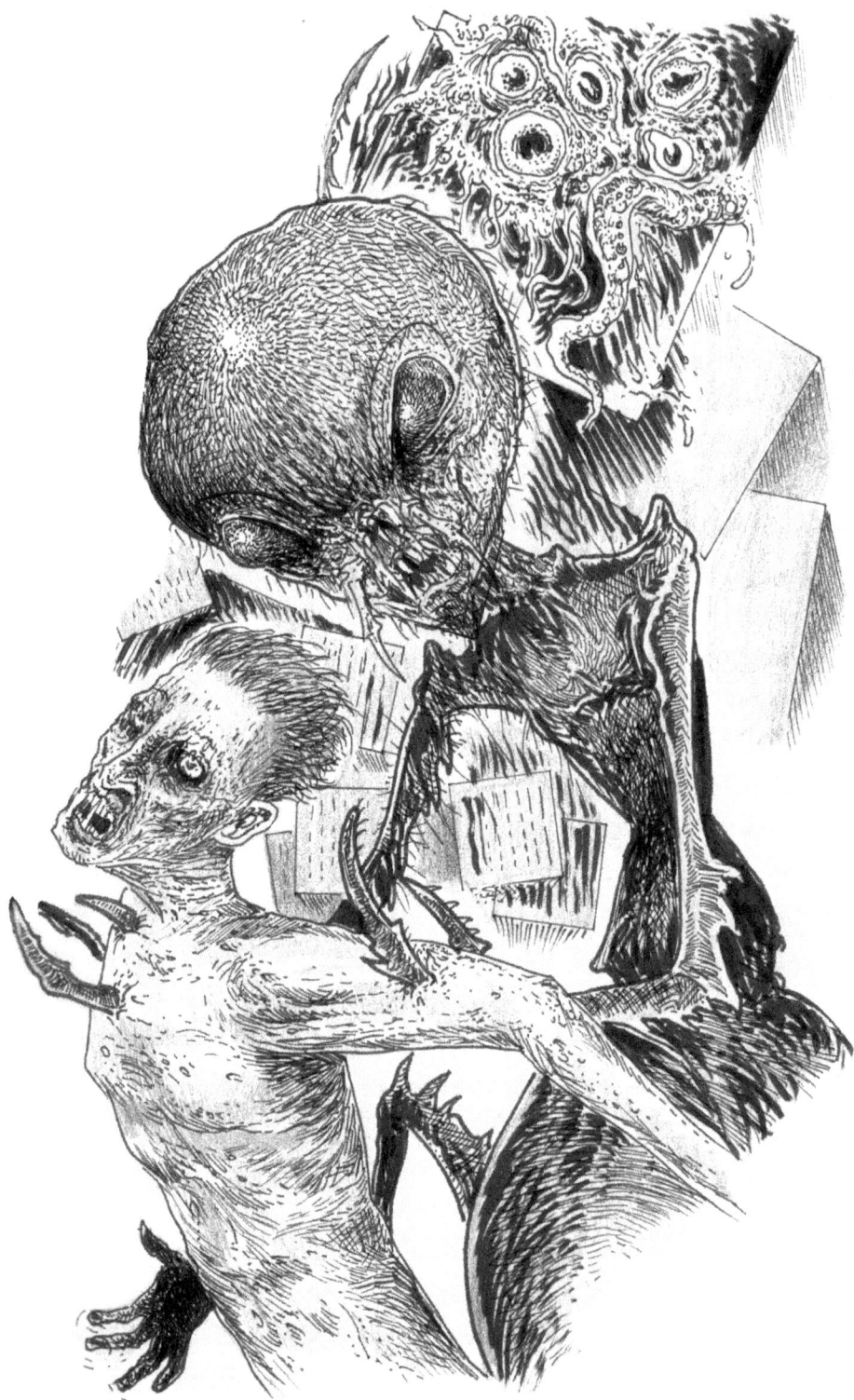